SIDELONG GLANCES

POEMS
by
MARY HUBBLE

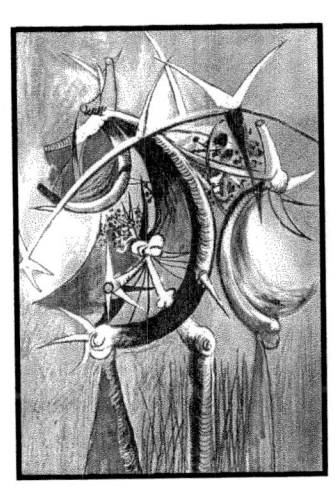

© Mary Hubble, 2001

No poems from this collection may be reproduced without permission from the author.

Some of these poems first appeared in:-

Envoi
Poetry Monthly
Poetry Digest
Poetry Nottingham International
The Seafarer
Perceptions
Norwich Competition-winners Anthologies
Manchester Cathedral Competition Anthology 2000

Cover illustration taken from *Thorn Heads* by Graham Sutherland, (1946).

ISBN 0 9531160 2 6

Published and printed by: PLUSH PUBLISHING, Plush, Dorchester, Dorset, DT2 7RJ

The Poems

The Last Veteran	1
Siblings	2
The Bridesmaid	4
The Third Death	6
Wearing Funny Hats	7
Leaving Charlie at the Nursery	8

~~~~~~~~~~~~

The Link	9
Portuguese Hot Pokers	10
Unmingling the Rubbish	11
Looking for Lalique in Lisbon	12
In a Spanish Square, at evening	14

~~~~~~~~~~~~

The Real Salome	16
The Gadarene Swineherd	18
I, Lazarus	20
The House at Capernaum	22
The Paralytic	24
The Woman taken in Adultery	26

~~~~~~~~~~~~

The Lie	27
Time to give up	28
The Sailor's Telegraph Pole	29
Unhappy New Year	30
Keeping a Clear Conscience	31
Her Ladyship	

~~~~~~~~~~~~

The Last Veteran

My father was a man of steeple height,
A silhouette against my childhood sky.
Sometimes casting shadows, sometimes shedding light,
He held me as the apple of his eye.

Before my birth he had known frantic fear,
Sent to do battle in a world gone mad.
He prayed each night for strength to persevere,
And carried with him Housman's *Shropshire Lad*.

He taught me fortitude and ways of grace,
How to use words and recognise bird-song,
To clean and leave the garden tools in place,
Not to boil plums or cabbages too long.

Crane's legs neatly clipped, yellow-caped when wet,
He rode each day to earn our daily bread,
Dutiful, precise, mindful of the debt
He felt he owed his Maker and his Dead.

For had he not survived Gallipoli?
Watched others die, unscathed come through that hell,
Returned to love and marry happily?
His mortgaged life must surely be lived well.

And well he lived it till his ninetieth year,
Still steeple-tall, on crane's legs, loved by all.
He faced his Maker without hint of fear,
Answering at last Gallipoli's bugle-call.

Siblings

We were always too far apart -
You, a skinny six year old
When our mother told you the news:
"A little sister or brother on the way
For you to love and cherish."
You tried, but what a bore I must have been!
Too young to play with, stealing time
Away from your prior claims. No wonder
You became withdrawn and took to kicking the cat.

Later, you would sometimes confide
Sins and secrets, and I would tell,
All innocence, not meaning to betray,
Bringing down punishment and breeding guilt.
Precocious girls at school feigned friendship,
Wangled access, and experimented
With you on the bed-settee while I kept watch.

Then came the call-up papers,
Uniform, and embarkation leave.
During your absence, I changed shape,
And when you did at last return, disarmed,
Bearing green bananas and a bent trombone,
Our meeting was a shock to both of us.

Art college, jazz, parental disapproval,
Beer, fags, out late at night -
Your six years' start left me lagging,
A watcher on the shore while you struck out.

Two wrecked marriages and several children later,
I caught you up, and we floundered together
In newfound congenial waters.
Close at last, perhaps too close,
Recalling sins and secrets, innocent no longer.

Death put an end to that little game.
The fags and beer combined to do you in.
That was six years since, and now I wonder -
Are you waiting to blow your bent trombone
And welcome me with green bananas
On a safer, sinless shore?

The Bridesmaid

A duplicate in summer-blue brocade,
I stand beside the sister of the bride.
We smile in unison, she undismayed,
While my sweet lips their secret venom hide.

Unwilling actor with a leading part
In this rehearsed and formalised charade,
I take great pains to screen my savage heart
Behind a careless air, a bright facade.

Offering dainties, smiling now, I flit
Among the guests. "You'll be next," they say,
Taking a vol-au-vent or fruit cream-split,
"A nice young man will come for you one day."

Until that flim-flam floosie stole him,
My brother was my chosen nice young man.
How cleverly I could cajole him
Within our cosy parent-powered clan,

To be my squire, my slave, my willing
Complice in every little cunning play
My scheming brain devised for filling
His leisure, so he'd never want to stray.

Now she has poached him with her landing-net,
And he, poor fish, is dished up, unaware.
See how he smiles and holds his glass to let
Me know that I am special still. Prepare

For pain, dear brother. My barbed hooks go deep.
She will pull you with her baited line,
But I will tear your flesh and make you leap
Back into my murky pool. You are mine.

Today I'll offer dainties, even so;
Play the sweet sister, raise my glass to all,
But like the cruel witch of long ago,
Without mercy, I'll have you in my thrall.

The Third Death

They say deaths come in threes,
So when two members of our circle
Dropped hands and stopped playing,
I became uneasy. Who next?
Interrupted by fears that tears
Would not end here, my grief
Snuffed the air for one more death.
The scent seemed close. Could it be
My destiny to make the triangle complete?
No. The scythe made a close shave,
Taking one very near and dear.
Six years' start he had on me
In life's race, born to our parents first,
Always there, until that awful day
When news came of the third death.
Now I can cease the anxious speculation.
For a while there will be no way
Through for the Grim Reaper. He has been
Three times, as they say.

Wearing funny hats

If ever there was an ugly duckling,
You were it. We had to laugh
At your no-chin, no-neck babyhood,
So you laughed back, bug-eyes bulging,
Hair sprouting like bleached grass.
We even put you in funny hats
To heighten the comic effect,
And lay back, helpless with laughter and love.

It has taken only two short years
For you to become a swan.
Now you are a stunner, turning heads
Wherever you go. We do not laugh.
Puzzled, you find a funny hat
And perch it on your golden curls,
Smiling above a perfect chin,
Bright eyes expectant, almost flirting.
Such beauty carries shades
Of Cleopatra, Helen of Troy,
Garbo, Marilyn, Diana -
What sort of future will it bring?

Leaving Charlie at the Nursery

Today he makes a fuss, pulls on my arm,
Drags his shoes, bawls like a young bull.
We approach the gate; other mothers stare.
Perhaps he's ill. Should I relent?
Suddenly he drops my hand, and head down
Charges in among the throng.
That's my brave boy! I escape,
Free to hurry home alone.
Without this respite, I am sunk.
Undiluted motherhood does not suit
My temperament. My mother was the same.
Only now can I forgive her cruel
Abandonement of me to other hands.
I hope my Charlie one day understands.

~~~~~~~~~~

The Link

Waiting for wine at noon
On a pavement in Portugal,
I am suddenly aware of a presence -
Not a beggar, though they are everywhere,
But a dark-clad, one-legged old man,
Self-propelled in a steel wheelchair.

His olive eyes stare not at me, nor at my purse,
But at the sleeping grandson by my side,
Safe in his own luxury wheeled transport.

Pointing with a simian hand engrained
As blackly as his empty trouser-leg,
He smiles, shrugs, indicates dumbly
His wry amusement at the link.
- Both he and this blond baby boy
Are helpless without wheels.

I nod and smile, sorry I cannot speak
His language. Using eloquent hands again,
He pays me the compliment
Of seeing a family likeness.
Then he strokes the sleeping head
And deftly steers himself away.

Portuguese Hot Pokers

Even the flowers play tricks
Here, where nothing is quite the same.
Ants are smaller, dogs fiercer,
Street-names longer, set in fancy tiles.

And just when you think you know
For sure the name of a flower,
It turns out to be different again.

"Red Hot Pokers," you cry, insistent,
Pointing to the tall orange spikes.
But no, not really. Here they are called
Something else. Not Red Hot Pokers.

You stand and stare, unconvinced.
Flaming away towards the sea
They point up straight and stiff,
Just like their name should be.
"That's what I'll call them, anyway," you whisper,
Not daring to touch in case they burn.

Unmingling the Rubbish

In the street where we live,
The dustbins are emptied every day.
Ours is often full, so we are glad.
Children make a lot of rubbish,
- Uneaten food, old clothes, broken toys.
We don't want it festering nearby,
Attracting flies and smelling bad.

"Where does it go?" you ask,
Watching the grey lorry drive away.
"Do they throw it in the sea?"
Surely not, but where else?
We have seen no incinerators
In this townscape, no landfill sites;
Sometimes a disfiguring dump
Off the main road, as if left by gypsies.
Could this be where it ends up?

We ask our daily help, a lady
Of great value. She knows everything.
"We unmingle," she says, dignified and proud.
Horrified, we turn away. So that's it.
Scavengers sift through our dross,
Eating out left-overs, wearing our rags,
Re-moulding our plastic bottles,
Sleeping on our old mattresses.

Now, we carefully sort out the food
From the rest, separate the rags,
Burn the nastiest bits.
This is the least we can do.

Looking for Lalique in Lisbon

Boldly I set out alone for Lisbon,
That celestial city lapped by a Sea of Straw.
Armed with map and shady hat,
I make erratic way along the river walk
To Black Horse Square and grid-planned streets
Where decorated pavements stretch ahead.
Then, leaving the Alfama
And St George's Castle for another day,
I press on past the Rossio
To tread the Avenidas leading north.

Straight lines on maps seem simple,
But with molten sun above
And burning stones beneath, one soon becomes
Misled. I wander from the narrow way,
Thinking to find a cooler route, like Bunyan's Pilgrim
Only to be caught in a snarer's net of streets
Taking me away from Heaven's Gate.

Despairingly I pray for help,
And am sent a wide-hipped angel
Carrying a basket of fresh fish.
"Gulbenkian," I plead, pointing to the map.
She takes my hand, silent but sure,
And leads me through a mini-maze to where
I wish to be. Thank God. I enter Paradise
To float through air-conditioned galleries
In company with quiet souls
All seeking beauty and enlightenment.

Past paintings, sculpture, tapestries,
Coins, jewels, porcelain, carved jade,
In mounting ecstasy I go
Until a promised treat comes near -
Glass by Lalique, my hero of the Art Nouveau.
But something horrid bars my way!
A polyglot display-board clearly states:
"This room is being rearranged
So it is closed today."

Banished from Paradise, I take a taxi back
To Purgatorial Portugal in June,
Cheated of that ultimate delight -
A Lalique dragonfly in jewelled flight.

In a Spanish Square, at evening

Angular, pale, familial,
Three figures near a café door,
Grouped like tired acrobats,
Stir and prepare their act.

The man sits on a metal chair,
Eyes closed, head tilted back,
Offering his face as canvas
For the woman's artistry.
She mixes greasepaint in a bowl,
Watched by her crippled boy.

Deftly she turns pale cheeks more pale,
Darkens dark brows to startling black;
Widow-peaked, his hair takes on
The semblance of a mourning cap.
Transformed, he climbs upon the chair
And stands balanced, immobile.

Expecting a show, we linger there.
Will he sing? Will she dance?
Maybe the lame boy will walk
On his hands or crablike, for laughs.
But no-one moves. Wife and son watch
The man keep still. This *is* the show.

For full four minutes he remains
Static. Newcomers to the square
Take him for a dummy and walk by.
Then someone throws a chinking coin.
He jerks, robotic, mechanical,
A metal automaton.

Between coin-drops he holds each pose,
As lifeless as a statue on a plinth,
Nor blinks nor breathes,
Though some do try to break his spell.
As time goes on the wonder grows
At such control, such grace, such skill.

Played out at last, he stops the game,
Climbs down, becomes soft flesh again.
They gather coins, replace the chair,
And make a quiet exit from the square.
Picasso would have painted them in blue,
Angular, pale, familial.

~~~~~~~~~~~~

The Real Salome
(St Mark's Gospel, Chapter 6, Verses 17-28)

All I did was try to please my mother.
She was the one who caused the strife,
Taking me with her when she married Father's brother,
Who had for her divorced his own first wife.
Their conduct roused the wrath of Holy John;
He told King Herod that he had no right
To Mother, or to me, or anyone
From Father's household, in God's sight.

Undaunted, Herod held a birthday feast,
And I was called to entertain his friends.
Shedding constraint, I danced, released
Like a wild bird that to the sun ascends.
The guests applauded me till they were tired.
King Herod promised me a prize;
Swore he would grant whatever I desired.
I ran and begged my mother to advise.

"Ask for the head of Holy John," she said,
Pinching my arm, pretending fond embrace.
"I'll have no peace till he is dead.
Do as I say or suffer vile disgrace."
I went back to the feasting king,
And contrary to my own true will,
Made my request for that so gruesome thing.

Herod did not want the death
Of John, rather that he might live,
Yet when he swore to me on oath
I knew whatever I should ask, he'd give.
So he sent a soldier of the guard
To grant my mother's envious wish,
And soon I got my grim reward,
Hideous, upon a dripping dish.

The eyes were glazed, the lips drawn back,
The hair hung down in disarray,
And from the gaping, jagged neck
Blood oozed and slopped and leaked away.
With all my strength I bore its weight
Before me through the crowded hall
To where my mother sat in state,
Waiting, triumphant, watched by all.

And as I saw her smile, thin-lipped,
With never a grateful look for me,
My arm jerked, and the dish I tipped,
Head, blood and hair, onto her knee.
"Here is my prize," I cried, "For you.
Take it, and may it please you well.
You see it as your rightful due,
I see it as your way to Hell."

The Gadarene Swineherd
(St Mark, Chapter 5, Verses 1-16)

Two thousand pigs was an exaggeration.
- More like two hundred I would say.
Our job was to guard and feed them,
Sharing their shelter night and day.

We were men who lived like pigs,
But bore our charges no ill-will;
They were our brothers, gentle friendly creatures,
Rooting and grunting on their native hill.

A madman lived among the tombs,
Naked and cut by chains and stones.
He screamed obscenities, robbed us of sleep,
And scratched in the dirt for stinking bones.

The pigs steered clear, sensing his torment,
Until a man called Jesus came,
Crossing the lake with many friends.
He asked the madman for his name.

"My name is Legion," he replied,
Forcing this Jesus to look him in the face.
A bargain of some sort was struck between them,
And suddenly our pigs began to race.

They shoved each other, quite unlike their custom,
Then down the slope into the lake they rolled,
A squealing mass of hooves and tails and snouts,
Awful and distressing to behold.

That Jesus had no word of cheer for us;
The madman was his chief concern.
Clothed and lucid, Legion sat beside him,
Miraculous proof of sanity's return.

All very well, except for our poor pigs.
Could Jesus not have found some other way?
Starvation threatens now our jobs are gone.
Will someone listen if we pray?

I, Lazarus

(St John's Gospel, Chapter 11, Verses 1-44)

My sisters sent a message, asking him to come,
But though he called himself our friend,
He wasted two more days across the river,
Talking in riddles of my likely end,
Before he travelled back to Bethany.

I died. There were no two ways about it.
The sweat, the pain, the blood, the mess
Gave no-one any cause to doubt it.
Blackness blotted out my sisters' grieving faces,
And that was all. I went nowhere;
Nowhere except into that smelly tomb.
Four days I lay and rotted there,
Until, to prove a point, he called me out,
And I came forth, trailing stained grave-clothes,
In grim obedient answer to his shout,
Raised up to glorify the son of God.

Others had been cured or revived,
But no-one raised when dead four days.
I was his biggest miracle so far,
A spectacle to illustrate his holy ways.

Washed, beside dear Martha and sweet Mary,
I sit, pretending to be glad of life.
But I am filled with awful dread,
For now I know that there is nothing
After death for me. I have been dead.

The House at Capernaum
(St Mark's Gospel, Chapter 1, Verses 16-35)

Before he called them from their nets
To fish for men, we lived in harmony,
My daughter and her spouse,
Their brother Andrew and myself.
Close neighbours James and John
Joined us for wine and evening talk,
And we were well content.

Then he passed by and marked them for his own.

Trailing to the synagogue to hear him teach
Was not my way. Nor did I like to watch
While madmen rolled and shrieked or cripples ran.
Rest was what I craved, and quiet,
So I retired to bed and let them go.
No sooner had I closed my eyes
Than back they all came to our house,
Led by my son-in-law, who told him:
"My wife's mother often waits on us
But now she has a fever and must sleep."
Sensing my deceit, he raised me up.
"Come, daughter, you are needed here."
Ashamed, I set about my tasks.
"A miracle!" the neighbours cried, and stayed
For hours, crowded round our door.

They brought their relatives for him to heal,
And all the time I slaved away
Providing food and clearing up the mess.
Then, would you believe, he stayed the night,
Choosing to use my bed.
Fresh sheets I spread, and joined my daughter on her couch,
Half-dead from weariness.

Now alone I keep the empty house,
Supported by a miracle.
Still fresh, the sheets his body touched
Bring perfect rest each night to my old bones.

The Paralytic
(St Mark's Gospel, Chapter 2, Verses 1-12)

I blessed the day my limbs lost strength,
My tongue its speech, for then no man
Could prove my guilt. I slept secure
Until a preacher came with healing powers.

For pity's sake four well-intentioned friends
Carried me through narrow streets
Towards a house so crammed with folk
That entry was impossible.
Relieved, I struggled to convey desire
For home, but they mistook my moans
And set their wits to getting me inside.

Observing that the roof was flat,
They dragged me up and made a hole
Through tile and thatch so they could lower me
To where he stood preaching the word.
Somehow he saw my soul laid bare,
But also saw the faith of my four friends.

"Son, your sins are forgiven," he declared.
Then, to prove supreme authority
Over accusing lawyers sitting near,
Added the command: "Take up your bed."
Obediently, I braved the crowd
And made my unaccustomed way back home.

I should be glad, but dread the days ahead.
Can I learn to walk a narrow path,
Or will my nature turn this second chance
Into a twice-told tale of woe?

The Woman Taken in Adultery
(St John's Gospel, Chapter 8, Verses 1-11)

They caught us together in the olive grove,
And dragged me, dishevelled, up to the temple.
(Him they ignored, as he did not suit their purpose.)
"See," they cried, making me stand in their midst,
"Caught in the very act. What do you think about that?"

He seemed to dream, scribbling in the dust,
So they pressed him, and he looked up.
Such a look! Burning yet from my lover's touch,
I flamed again and shuddered with desire.
"Should she be stoned?" they urged.
Still looking, he sat up straight.
"Let him who has no sin throw the first stone."
Then he returned to his scribbling.

One by one they crept away, shamed,
Till none was left in all that space.
I could have run, but stayed, yearning.
Again that look, and then I knew.
No other lover would have me in the olive grove;
No lover would ever have me more,
For I was his, body and soul.

~~~~~~~~~~~~

[26]

The Lie

Such a little lie she told him,
Not knowing just how much it meant.
"I love sailing. The sea is in my blood."
He, who had been seeking the perfect crew
To help him weather life's storms,
Thought he had found his heart's desire.

"I've made my own boat," he told her proudly.
"It's waiting in the marina, all ready to go."
She stepped aboard, but not until
They were far out in the bay
Did she confess that she loved
The idea of sailing, but suffered
Horribly from seasickness,
So please could they remain on shore?

His heart sank like an anchor
As he steered them back to land.
Her lie had trapped them in a prison-hulk
Of slime and rotting timbers.

Time to give up

If I should see your face again
Across a crowded café floor
Or through a misted window-pane,
Could I be really sure
I had remembered right?
Age can be a deep disguise;
For all my certainty, I might
Mistake for you some stranger who
Resembled you as once you were.
How foolish it would be for me
To call or wave or run to her
And see, when close, her hostile eyes
Reflecting back my shocked surprise.

So while I can I here decide
That should I ever meet a stare
Which could be yours, I'll turn aside
And not pursue the search for you,
Pretending I'm too old to care.

The Sailor's Telegraph Pole

Above this hostile sea of tile and stone,
My fan-rigged mast serves as a trusted guide,
A landmark when I voyage out alone,
Confused by ceaseless traffic's swirling tide.
I trade with friendly craft in clean dry docks,
Avoiding caves where thieving pirates roam,
Then turn past flower-filled islands hemmed by rocks
And take strict bearings for the journey home.
My beacon pointing to the sky shows clear
Against all densities of dark or light;
I cannot miss the harbour as I steer,
Keeping that constant marker in my sight.

If ever storm should blow my safeguard down,
I'll quit this God-forsaken land-locked town.

Unhappy New Year

We sat together, three tired women
Waiting for an old year's end
And a new one's beginning.
Each clutched a full glass
In sore, big-knuckled hands,
Wondering what to drink to.
Absent friends? Long-dead lovers?

Tedious talk tossed to and fro
Like ping-pong in slow motion.
Spoilsports, we let balls go by,
Wanting the game to finish.
Someone turned on "Lottery Live",
Engendering a momentary thrill,

But our numbers did not come up -
We never have real hope they will.
Midnight still far off, we crept to bed,
United in our fear of Auld Lang Syne.
For us, one year was very like another;
What had we to celebrate?
But there was no escape,
For we were woken later
By fireworks and a peal of bells.

Keeping a Clear Conscience

Each day, I brave the underpass
Armed with a coin for one who waits
Half-way along, beside his plastic cup.
Sometimes a blanket cushions him from cold,
But often he sits careless on bare stone.

He is not old, or crippled, or insane,
Does not leap up, or shout, or cause offence.
Huddled and quiet, he simply sits,
Available for those whose consciences
Are raw from watching horrors on the screen.

His cup is near for us to fill
If Africa or India
Are too remote for our direct concern.
How would I feel if one day he is found
Not sitting on cold stone, but lying prone?

I'll seek another beggar when he goes,
Another plastic cup for my largesse.
How else can I pursue my way,
Fortunate, virtuous, correct,
My duty done, my conscience clear?

Her Ladyship

After a stormy passage,
With wrecks and rocks and rollers
Hampering her way,
She is anchored safe
In a secluded harbour,
Alone but not stranded.
Her battered figurehead looks forward
Above sound timbers and an even keel.

She rides serenely on the swell
Caused by other vessels
Setting out again to sea.
They will meet pirates,
Suffer torn sails, smashed masts;
Lose direction, take in water,
Maybe sink with all hands,
While she stays here, snug-berthed, shipshape.